DIARY OF A BLANK EMOJI
BOOK 1 - EMOJI ACADEMY

BY BLANK THE EMOJI

Disclaimer

Blank the Emoji © Copyright 2017

All rights reserved.

This is a work of fiction. Names, characters, places and incidents are either products of the author's imaginations or used fictitiously. Any resemblance to actual events, locales or persons, living or dead, is entirely coincidental.

No part of this publication may be reproduced or transmitted in any form by any means, electronic or mechanic, without permission in writing from the author.

First Quarter

September 2nd, 2015: 7:53 p.m.

I've just started my own diary with the Center's writing app. They said that I needed to write until I can make a face. They think it will help.

All of my friends have already gone into the latest update and been installed. Smirk, Winky and even Crybaby. They passed all of their classes and now they're with all the other current Emoji. Dad says that I'll have my time soon enough.

He thinks that things will change, and somehow I'll be accepted into the system. But what does he know? He's outdated and old-fashioned. He comes from a time when you had to literally work out how to type your name in as few characters as possible. It was easier back then. When all you had to be was :P. It must have been a cinch to get through.

Today was the first day of school again. This will be my second time going through Emoji Academy. And this time everyone already knows who I am, and why I wasn't accepted. An Emoji without an expression is like a phone that hasn't been charged. It just doesn't work. That's the analogy Mr. Smiley always uses, anyway.

"Blank?" Mr. Smiley said as he took role. He was the oldest Emoji ever. No one knows how he came to be--whether he created himself, or if there was another. The only thing we all know is that he's been here the longest. There hasn't been a successfully updated and used Emoji who wasn't taught by Mr. Smiley

"Here," I mumbled, and there was a murmuring that moved through the room like a whispering wave. I wanted to be anywhere else than back in my seat in the front row of class. I had already gone through all of this. And I was completely, one-hundred-and-ten-percent positive that I would fail all my classes yet again.

Mr. Smiley finished taking attendance and started right in on the very same introductory lecture that I heard last year. It was very inspirational and moving. Or it was the first time I had heard it. Now it sounded like a canned performance. I wondered if Mr. Smiley ever got bored teaching the same old class year after year. He went on and on about the Emoji's purpose to help the makers express themselves, and how no one should be ashamed of their true expressions.

"To each and every one of you I say this," he said, pacing back and forth in front of the class. "You will all find your face. It may take some time. You will have to work, and study, and try on a great many different faces to shape the one you were given when you were made. There is much to learn, but also much to take away…"

As he went on and on I could feel my eyes drooping and my head tilting downward. I didn't get much sleep the night before. Besides that, I knew the lecture Mr. Smiley was giving word for word. He made it at least a dozen times over the course of the last year. I could fill in the blanks well enough. Not that I thought it would do me any good. Isn't doing the same thing over and over the definition of insanity anyway?

"…however, this year we're going to be doing things slightly differently, given the circumstances."

I lifted my head. This was new.

Mr. Smiley smiled at the class, which wasn't all that new. What he said next was.

"I'm going to be putting you all into groups for the first quarter," he said. "And for our first project each group will carry out a conversation by using as many faces as they can already." He held up a hand at the groans of some in the back. "You will not be graded on the number of faces that you can make, or the quality. This is simply an exercise in communication. A little fun warm-up to kick off the year."

It sounded like the total opposite of fun. You see, when Emoji are born, they have a natural expression on, but it's imperfect and rough. Like a lump of Play-Doh. Emoji need to be shaped and crafted before they can have any hope of being uploaded. That's what Mr. Smiley calls 'finding your face'. To do that, most Emoji imitate other faces until they create their own, which is the polished version of the one they were born in.

The thing is, I can't imitate other faces. At all. I guess that's why they call me Blank.

I got placed into a group with two Emoji who couldn't be more different. The first one looked like some kind of robot that couldn't decide how big his knobs were, or the size and shape of his eyes, or what color he was painted.

"Call me Rob," he said. "Short for Robot."

The other looked like she could have been uploaded in the last update. She had an alien face and her chin came to a perfect point, but was round on the top. Her eyes were both the same size and shiny black.

"Ally," she said.

"Nice to meet you," I said. "I'm Blank."

At the end of the day Mr. Smiley called for me to hang back. I waited in front of his desk until everyone else had left.

"We're going to make this work, Blank," he said. "I want you to keep writing in your diary like we talked about last week with your parents. "This is the year we're going to get you your face, and you'll be uploaded soon enough. I've never had a student fail me."

And so here I am. Trying not to fail.

September 23rd, 2015: 4:12 p.m.

This whole group project isn't going so well.

There's no real problem with our group. Ally is great. She says her parents started teaching her as far back as she can remember. Rob's faces don't have the same polish to them, and usually he makes different versions of the same couple of goofy faces. But he still has a wide range of emotions he can express. The real problem is me.

"Why don't you try a simple smile?" Ally said earlier during class. "Like Mr. Smiley's, see?" She mimicked the expression perfectly on her alien face.

"What do you think I've been trying to do the past year?" I said. "I can't."

"That's it," Rob said. "We're going to fail the first project of the year. Great. I better not have to take an extra year too."

"We're not going to fail," Ally said. "We're just going to have to find a way to work Blank into a full conversation. That's all."

She said it like it was so simple. Basically, the two of them would have a conversation and I would be left staring into Mr. Smiley's judging eyes. It was probably our only option though. Time was running out, and we only had another month before the end of the quarter was here.

"Well we're going to have to think fast," Rob said.

We all put our heads together, and started to plan.

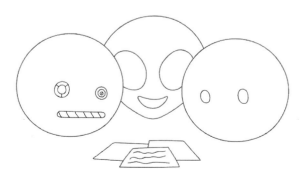

October 12, 2015: 1:26 p.m.

I went home early today. I told Mr. Smiley I wasn't feeling well, but really I just didn't want to practice our group presentation again.

It wasn't that we didn't have it planned out yet. The end of the semester was only two weeks away, so we had to come up with something. I just knew Mr. Smiley wasn't going to like it, because it involved me doing nothing more than blinking.

It goes like this: Ally comes up to me and gives a big smiley face. Then I blink, and her face switches to a frown. Then Rob comes up and gives a confused look, and Ally gives it right back. Rob makes a couple goofy faces at me that I blink at, and then they both just walk away. And that's the end.

The whole conversation is about how I can't do anything else but stare and blink. It's terrible, and maybe the most embarrassing thing in the world. All it does is single me out, and remind me of why I didn't get uploaded. It reminds me of how I'm different.

I couldn't take that anymore. Not after two straight weeks of practicing for the last hour of class every day. And all it was watching Ally and Rob practice and try and decide on which faces they would make. I just kept doing the same thing.

When I got home Dad asked me why I was back so early. I told him the same lie and just went to my bedroom. I didn't want to explain anything to anybody. So I came back and started writing.

The truth is I don't really want to do anything. Especially not go back to school tomorrow.

October 23rd, 2015: 6:06 p.m.

Oh shoot, oh shoot, oh shoot.

Tomorrow is the group project and I really don't want to go. We've finished our discussion, and have it down to the last second. I tried to focus on the timing of my blinks, so that I can make them all as expressive as possible, but I'm not sure how well it comes across.

Ally and Rob both told me not to worry, and they're probably right. But they've been practicing their faces so much that they both have it down. Rob can even keep his other parts from moving, and they're all the same color, too. If we get individual grades, I'm the only one who will fail. And if we get a group grade, I'll be the only reason we fail.

They're good friends, but I'm afraid that at the end of the year the same thing is going to happen, and I'll lose them. That's how I lost Smirk and Winkie, and even Crybaby, who barely passed. I didn't want to lose my new friends too.

On the plus side I do feel like writing has been good for me. I feel a little more confident in class, even if all I can do is blink.

October 24th, 2015: 4:45 p.m.

The presentation didn't go quite as expected. But at least the quarter is over now.

When we got up to present I could feel my whole body fluttering. I thought I knew exactly what to expect. There would be a long, uncomfortably awkward silence, and then Mr. Smiley would call the next group politely, and hold me back after class again.

After my first blink there was a ripple of giggling throughout the class. I was glad my color couldn't change so I didn't turn red from embarrassment. At the next blink even Mr. Smiley let out a little chuckle. I was so embarrassed, and was sure we had failed at my first blink. But at the end of our presentation, the customary applause was louder than I expected it to be. Ally and Rob both flashed me big, toothy grins.

"Great job you all, "Mr. Smiley said. And he was clapping too.

At the end of class he still held me back. "I just want to say I appreciate you trying out there, giving it your all and everything. I could feel the expressions wanting to get out in your blinks. Your group managed to convey some humor. That's quite impressive for this early."

"Thanks." I couldn't tell if it was a compliment or not, but decided that if I treated it as one, then maybe he would too.

"Keep up the good work, Blank," he said. "One step at a time."

So maybe that means that I'm making progress. Then again, maybe Mr. Smiley is just saying that and hoping I'll find the inspiration to change by the end of the year.

Either way, I figure as long as I'm in his good graces, things can't be that bad.

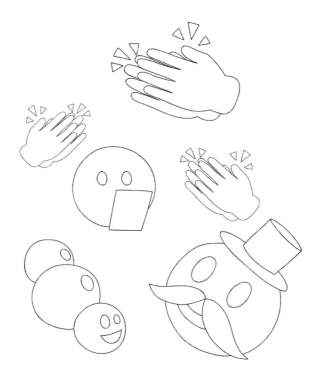

Second Quarter

October 27th, 2017: 5:15 p.m.

Today was the first day of the second quarter. Thankfully, Mr. Smiley didn't start the class with another announcement of a surprise group project. The lecture he gave was much more like the ones he gave all the time last year. His expression was more strained than usual. There were bags underneath his perky eyes. I think he falls back to these older lectures whenever he feels tired.

After lunch Mr. Smiley wiped the board and stood at the front of class. He cleared his throat, and the murmuring and giggling of the other students grew quiet.

"Now," he said. "I'm sure you all are aware of the holidays creeping up on us. Some are more near than others."

At this, several of the more colorful Emoji whooped and laughed. They were Seasonals, only to be used during the Holidays when they were eventually uploaded, and everyone else just hated them. They were all too happy about their own holiday, and sullen and grumpy during the off-season.

"Quiet down, now," said Mr. Smiley as he continued. "Yes, we all love the holiday season, which is why for each holiday left--that's three now: Halloween, Thanksgiving, and Christmas--we will be getting into the holiday spirit as much as we possibly can. How does that sound?"

The cheering came mostly from the Seasonals, but Ally and Rob clapped too. I looked at Ally and she gave a half-shrug and mouthed *Sorry* to me. I didn't clap. To me the holidays always seem like just another time of year when I would be singled out for not showing any emotion. So get the mistletoe hung and the chestnuts roasting. It made very little difference to me.

"So for each holiday this year, we'll be having, you guessed it, a party to properly celebrate each occasion." There were a couple more whoops from some of the Seasonals at this, but Mr. Smiley raised a hand for silence. "I want you all to get as festive as possible, and so we'll be putting on a costume party for Halloween, the nearest holiday. We'll celebrate with a little party on Monday, so over the weekend, I would encourage you all to work your hardest and bring your A-game."

October 28th, 2015: 11:27 a.m.

I asked my dad for help with making my Halloween costume. I had no idea what I was going to be, or even what I could be. The options seemed pretty limited, to be honest.

"Let's try this," my dad said, and walked down the stairs to the laundry room. He came back moments later with a blank white sheet, and set it down on the table in the dining room. Then he rummaged around some drawers until he came up with a pair of scissors. He then cut out to large eye-holes in the middle of the sheet, stood up, and draped the whole thing over me.

My vision was briefly clouded underneath the blanket of white. I could see the shadow of my dad through the light that streamed in. "I can't see anything," I said to him.

"Whoop, here we go," he said, and shifted the sheet around so that the eye-holes matched up with my eyes. The left one was a little too small, and I could only see about half as much through it as my right. "There," he said. "What do you think?"

"What am I?"

"A ghost! Boo! Ha-ha."

I walked to the bathroom to look at myself in the mirror. I was underwhelmed, to say the least. Two eyes on a blank face, I basically still looked like myself. At least everyone would be able to recognize me, I thought. It was a small condolence.

As I came out of the bathroom my dad was standing there waiting outside the door. He looked so happy and proud that I didn't want to disappoint him. "Well?" he said. "What do you think?"

"It's great," I lied.

"Really? You like it? I wore one just like it when I was your age."

Parents, as a rule, know exactly what the worst thing to say is. And they always seem to just say it anyway. That was one of the few moments when I was glad that I couldn't show my expression on my face. "Cool," I said.

That night I talked to Ally over chat in my room, and I told her the whole story.

"It can't be that bad if your dad's done it before though, right?" she said. "At least you know it'll work."

"That's what he told me," I said. "But that was years ago. And it's not even scary or anything. For all I know he could just be lying to me, just to make me feel better."

"Isn't that what you were doing when you told him you liked it?"

"Yeah, I guess so. What are you going as?"

"A zombie alien," she said. "I managed to spook my mom when she woke up." Ally giggled. "She was pretty scared."

We chatted for a little while longer, talking about the looming finals at the end of the semester, and wondering what they would test us on. I was sure that they would change it up from last years, which had a multiple choice Emoji recognition portion, as well as an on-the-spot performance of each expression you had mastered. I failed last year on the performance section, but nailed the written test. Too bad 50% is still a failing grade.

After we were done talking I lay down on my bed for a while. Fears and concerns and negative thoughts poured into my mind and threatened to scare me away from trying. Don't go back to school, they said. You'll never make it as a real Emoji. You can't even smile.

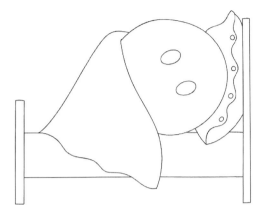

I stood up quickly and went to get my tablet for another journal entry. One thing Mr. Smiley told me when giving me the tablet was that I should write whenever I felt bad, and keep writing until it was all out. Well I did, and I do feel a little better. If I never make it as an Emoji, then at least my journal will survive. Then maybe someone else like me can read it, and maybe learn something that I didn't.

October 31st, 2015: 5:15 p.m.

So today was the Halloween party, and I have to say that I think I might be getting the hang of things this time around. I've definitely stopped caring about what other people think of me. That's either a good thing, or it'll lead me to another year of Emoji Academy. Only time will tell.

I decided to stick with the ghost costume Dad gave me after all. For a while I was thinking about trying to make my own, but I couldn't come up with anything scary or funny to go with my blank face.

Almost everyone at the party was dressed to scare. There were spooky witches, groaning zombies, grinning werewolves and more. Ally's zombie alien face was really good, and gave me a jump the first time I saw her. Rob turned his eyes read to be a killer robot from outer space. It was pretty good, but as with any of the faces Rob made, I couldn't help but laugh.

"Hey at least it's scarier than you," he said. "What are you supposed to be, anyway?"

"A ghost," I said, still laughing. I knew my costume was worse than any of the others, but I was still having a good time. "Boo!"

Rob laughed. "I'm shaking," he said.

Mr. Smiley set up a table with punch and snacks, and for the first hour of class we all ate and talked and walked around, looking at everyone else's costumes. There was a lot of laughing, and a lot of congratulatory exchanges on particularly good costume arrangements. I found that my costume was getting noticed more and more as the party went on. Most people started off confused, but I could usually get them to laugh with another, "Boo!" like the ones my dad gave me.

"What a great costume, Blank!" Mr. Smiley said when I went up for some more punch. "Very funny. You surprised me."

"Thanks, Mr. Smiley," I said, feeling the warm glow of pride spreading inside. "My dad helped me make it."

"Well he did a very good job. How is the writing going?"

"Good. I think it's really helping me."

"That's good to hear. I can see you've already made some progress."

Hearing that from Mr. Smiley felt better than anything else this year has. Things are starting to look up now, I think. I'm starting to feel more like one of the members of the class. I remember last year at this same time I was always sitting at the back of class alone. I wouldn't talk to anyone, because I didn't want any of them to think that i was different from then. But I also didn't try to be like them, either. I think writing in this journal has helped me to look at the things I do day by day, and see why I do them. I feel like I'm starting to get to know myself better.

After the long day of games and fun at the party, I'm really looking forward to the next one. Maybe I could make a run at being a holiday emoji by the end of the year. It's just a thought.

November 2nd, 2015: 6:20 p.m.

Today Mr. Smiley let us know what to look forward to for the next holiday party. Halloween was already over and Thanksgiving was coming up fast. At least that was how he put it. Three weeks still seemed like a long way off to me.

"As we all know, Thanksgiving is about food. The users eat the food, and it is our duty to show and describe it all. So I want you to all think about what food or dish you would be, if you were one. Try to pick something that describes your own personality."

When I heard that I knew I was in trouble. How was I supposed to describe my own personality, when I didn't even know what that was? Could I just go with the turkey, and leave it at that? How much would I have to explain? I brushed off the questions and the doubt. I was still feeling pretty good about how Halloween went, and was sure that I would come up with something.

November 9th, 2015: 8:33 p.m.

Still haven't figured out what dish I'm going to be for the Thanksgiving party. School hasn't been going so well lately. I'm not doing as well on some of the same homework assignments I had last year and it's starting to get to me. I do fine with the facial recognition worksheets, but I still frequently make mistakes when answering the 'real-world' problems. I can never think about what face should be used in any of the scenarios, and sometimes I just end up leaving them blank.

Ally already has hers picked out, and as usual it's spot on. She's choosing a variation of stuffing with sticky rice in it, and pointing out that what they share in common is their foreignness. She's always so clever with hers.

Rob still hasn't chosen one, which made me feel better when I asked him about it.

"It's either canned cranberry sauce or stuffing," he said. When I asked him why, he told me, "Because those are the silliest two dishes. What are they even?"

I'm sure I'll find a dish of my own. There's still plenty of time, after all. The only thing I do wish is that once the holiday season is over we won't be getting so many assignments and projects!

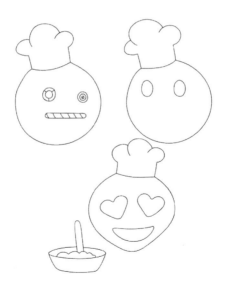

November 17th, 2015: 4:13 p.m.

Well, I've finally picked out my dish, and I definitely LOL'd when I thought of it. I'm going to choose mashed potatoes, because they're the most like me. They're plain.

November 24th, 2015: 8:43 p.m.

Today was the Thanksgiving party, if you can even call it that. Thanksgiving is never as big of a holiday as Halloween or Christmas, almost as a rule. And so Mr. Smiley made sure that our celebration reflected that. At the start of class, we all stayed in our seats, and went around saying what our foods were.

When it was my turn, I said, "Mashed potatoes, because they're plain, like me."

A few of the Seasonals snickered in their seats, and Mr. Smiley waved a hand to quiet them down. He motioned for me to continue. "That's all well and good, Blank," he said. "But try and be a little more descriptive."

My cheeks were burning. Everyone else had only said one or two things. I didn't know why I was being put on the spot. I shook my head, and said, "No, that's all."

"I see," said Mr. Smiley.

The second emoji after me chose mashed potatoes too. And when he gave his reason, he said, "Because you can smash them into any shape, and I can do that with my face, watch." He demonstrated by showing a squinting face with pointy eyebrows.

Mr. Smiley clapped and exclaimed, "That's great! Such imagination." And as we moved on to the next student he glanced my way. It was only for a second, but I knew that he was wondering whether or not I would actually turn out any different this year.

December 3rd, 2015: 1:56 p.m.

I haven't been writing in my journal lately. This is the first time I've written in over a week. I'm in a better mood today than I have been lately. Probably all due to the news Mr. Smiley gave us all today.

We had been waiting for word on what the next holiday project would be. Since it was nearing the end of the quarter, I thought it was going to be a big one. I'm happy to say that I couldn't have been more wrong.

"I'm sure you'll all be happy to hear the good news," Mr. Smiley said, looking around the room, "that the Christmas party this year will be having no additional assignments or projects attached to it. You have all worked hard for the past two quarters, and you deserve some much needed rest and relaxation."

A cheer went up through the classroom. It was the best news I had personally gotten all year. And I could see a lot of relieved faces as I looked around the room.

"Instead, we'll be having a dance."

December 11th, 2015: 6:03 p.m.

I had to pluck up all my courage today to ask Ally out to the Christmas dance.

I was going to ask her at lunch, but I forgot to bring mine from home, and had to stand in the long line for a bunch of unidentifiable slop. By the time I got to a table and started eating, I was in no mood to ask anybody anything.

So when I got home I decided that I would ask her over chat. It would be easier to do without her standing right there in front of me.

"What's up?" I typed on the tablet in my room.

"Nothing. Just finishing up some homework. You?"

"Same."

There was six minutes of silence then, which felt like the longest and deepest chasm ever. I decided to end it myself, and just get the rejection over with. I hoped we could still be friends."

"Do you want to go to the Christmas dance with me?"

Three minutes passed. Then, "Rob already asked me," she said.

I sunk my head. Of course. "That's cool." I said.

"I haven't told him yes or no yet."

"Well," I typed, heart pounding, "do you want to go with me instead?"

"Sure."

No four letters could ever be more beautiful. Sure. I was on cloud nine, but I couldn't show it. I had to play it cool.

"Alright cool," I said. "I've got to finish up this homework now, but I'll talk to you tomorrow."

"Goodnight," she said.

"Goodnight."

This year just keeps getting better and better.

December 21st, 2015: 4:13 p.m.

The dance was today. It had its ups and downs, I guess.

The biggest up was of course Ally.

The classroom had all of the chairs removed from it when we all walked into class that day. The lights were turned down low, and Christmas music was playing. Ally smiled at me when I walked in, but Rob wouldn't look me in the eyes. He was on the other side of the room, talking with some of Seasonals dressed as reindeer.

The party was good. There was plenty of tasty holiday food, and everything was red and gold. There was even mistletoe, but I steered Ally away from underneath it while we were dancing. I didn't want to kiss in front of everyone in the class. Everyone else must have felt the same, because its presence created a vacuum on the dance floor, where none dared tread.

After class Ally gave me a little kiss on the cheek. It was after everyone else was moving out of the room, so no one saw it happen. But it happened.

I didn't think I would ever say it, but I think it was the best thing ever that I didn't get uploaded last year.

Third Quarter

January 1st, 2016: 1:54 p.m.

Today is the first day of a new year. A new year in which I *know* that I will be graduating. It's my resolution, after all.

I got the results from the first semester in the mail a few days ago, and I got the highest grade possible. If things keep going this way, there's no way I'll be stopped from the next upload. Still, that doesn't mean that I'm too excited about classes starting again next week. The first semester seemed like it was mostly fun. I thought it was unlikely that Mr. Smiley would continue to go easy on all of us. But hey, I guess anything can happen, right?

The single best thing about break was being able to see Ally as much as I wanted. After the dance went so well, we started hanging out. Since I was a year older, and practically an adult by Emoji standards, we didn't have to just sit inside one of our parents' houses and play games or talk. After all, I did have access to the transport stream.

The transport stream is the only form of transportation available to Emoji. For example, one comes every day to pick me up from my home and take me to school. Travel is near instantaneous, so it doesn't take too long to pick everyone up day after day.

But since I didn't graduate, I was technically given free access to the stream. I don't even have to go back to school if I don't want to, but I would be forced to stay in my parents' home. They don't allow unretired or failed Emoji to gain their own quarters, which makes sense. That's why I'm going back to school, after all.

Anyway, since I have access to the stream, Ally and I were able to use it to explore. We went to the mall and did some window shopping since neither of us had any credits to buy anything. But that was okay. All I really wanted to do was just be with her. We held hands while we walked, and every now and then Ally would change her face to surprise me. She changed it to a man's face once, and had to chase me down the walkway when I turned and ran.

"Do you think you'll ever be able to do it yourself?" she asked, meaning would I ever be able to look like anything else but two dots on a yellow face.

"I don't know," I said, taking her hand again. I bumped against her playfully. "But if that's all I got, I guess that's what you're stuck with, right?"

Ally was quiet, and for a moment we were only walking. She seemed to be more interested in what was in the accessory stores that lined the walkway than continuing our conversation.

"What?" I asked.

"She stopped walking. "It's just," she said. "I'm still going to graduate at the end of the year. And if you don't graduate again, I don't know how we'll be able to stay together. We'll be on two complete opposite sides of the world."

Now it was my turn to go all quiet. We kept walking before I found the courage to answer. "So you wouldn't," I said, hearing my voice strain and hating myself for it. "You wouldn't stay here with me?"

"And what, we'd both keep living in our parents' houses until you finally graduate? I can't do that. If I get the chance, I'm going into the next upload."

I started to turn around. "Maybe it's time we head back," I said. "We told your parents we wouldn't be gone too long."

Then she just sighed and said, "Okay."

I took her back home then. That was just earlier today. That's why I had to come back and write. Nothing else felt like it would stop me from thinking about it too much. Sometimes writing out your thoughts is good for that. Then you can organize them for yourself, and get to what you were really feeling about when whatever happened to make you write in the first place. It's like a circle, and I'm not sure that I'll ever stop drawing it, now that I've started.

And that was how we left it. I haven't talked to Ally since I dropped her off. Granted, that was only a few hours ago, but it's definitely a change in pace from our nonstop messaging over most of break. I think I should give her some space. She'll message me if she wants to.

All of that being said, I think I've decided what I'm going to do about this big hiccup between me and Ally. That's the main reason why I made my resolution today. I'm going to graduate. And Ally and I will be together once we're both uploaded. Forever.

I haven't seen Rob at all during break, and now I feel bad about that. I hope he isn't too mad at me for asking Ally to the dance after he already did. I hope we can still be friends once school starts back up again.

I didn't have any friends last year. No one really wanted to talk to me. It was like they all thought that they would catch whatever sickness I had, and also be an outcast. I can understand why no one else would want to risk that. I had trouble enough living it every day.

But that's enough negativity. That was the past, and I can't change anything about it. The only thing that I can do is keep doing what I've been doing. Now more than ever. Failure isn't an option. I've just gotta pull myself together and do as well as I can in these next two quarters. Mr. Smiley believes in me, and I've got my journal if nothing else. Even if Rob and Ally both desert me, I have to keep going. I've got to remember that I'm doing this more for myself than anyone else.

But of course, as soon as I say that all I can see is Ally's face.

January 4th, 2016: 4:15 p.m.

The first day of the new semester couldn't have been more different from the last. For starters, neither Rob nor Ally said a word to me all day. Rob sat on the other side of the room from where he usually sat, and talked and joked with the Seasonals the whole day. I would sometimes catch his eye, but he would just turn away and talk to his new friends.

Ally didn't seem mad at me. She just looked sad. Still, like Rob she tried not to meet my gaze. We'd usually talk and whisper together throughout class, but today she seemed to be more interested in Mr. Smiley's lecture on the expressiveness of eyebrows.

"Apart from the mouth, there is no other component that can deliver as wide of a range and expressive of emotions like the eyebrows…"

I passed her a note after lunch. She didn't change her seat like Rob, so it was easy to lean over and drop it on her desk.

This is what the note said: *I'm sorry. Are we okay?*

I saw her bend down to open and read the note, but she didn't respond for another hour. Then she got my attention with a *psst,* and passed the note back.

Underneath my own scribbled message were these words: *I think so, but I don't know if we should keep seeing each other. I miss Rob.*

I felt a burning sensation rise up to my ears as I read the note over one more time. Of course. Rob. The one who she was probably now wishing she had gone with to the Christmas dance over me. At least with Rob she had a better chance of being with someone who would also graduate. I'm sure that's what she was thinking, and it hurt more than I expected it to.

I didn't answer her note back. At the end of the day I gathered up my things and made my way to the transport as fast as I could. I sat way in the back, put on my headphones, and listened to music the whole way back.

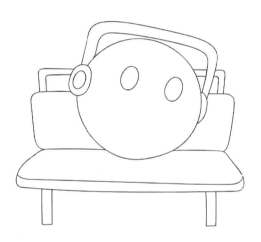

"How was school?" my Mom asked when I came in the door.

"Fine," I lied, and tried to walk past her to my room.

She stopped me with a gentle hand. "Hold on, cowboy," she said. "If you're anything like your father, then I know 'fine' really means something, you just don't think I'll understand. Am I right?"

I didn't say anything to her, but when she looked at me with the stern, concerned eyes of a mother, I nodded my head in defeat.

"That's just fine," she said. "You're old enough to figure out your own problems. I just want you to know that you can always come to me when something's wrong, and I promise to listen. Deal?"

I smiled, glad to have escaped explaining how I was feeling just then. "Deal."

What I was feeling, which I still haven't told anyone else, was a sense of worthlessness and loneliness. It seemed like I had just figured out how to live a normal life like any other Emoji, and now the dream was over and things were going back to normal.

What I've learned from this is that I can't rely on anyone else to help me get what I want. If I want to graduate I can't be distracted by the things that I can't have. I'll only be able to have real friends if I can graduate. Then maybe on the other side of the upload, Ally and I can be together again.

January 11th, 2016: 6:12 p.m.

Things have been going better lately. The fact that I haven't needed to write for a week should be a good enough sign of that. I've also been more busy than usual with all the extra work Mr. Smiley has started to give me. I'll go into that first.

On the third day of the new semester Mr. Smiley held me back from class again. He'd been doing this all year, a quick check up every now and then to see how I was feeling about the course load and if there was anything he could do to help. This time was different.

"Sit down a moment, Blank," he said, gesturing to one of the seats in the front row. I took a seat right in front of his desk, where he sat. "Now," he went on, "I know you're doing well so far, but we're going to begin to get into more of the same material you saw last year. I don't want you to be bored, but I was having some difficulty in figuring out what you could do different so that you would still be getting enough out of every class." He paused and raised an eyebrow at me.

I nodded to show that I was following him.

"What I have decided," he said. "Is that you will be my aide for this semester. You will help with grading all of the material--that will be a good substitute to homework, and towards the end of the quarter I may even have you lead a class. How does that sound?"

Frankly, it sounded terrible. I didn't know how to teach, and how could I be trusted to grade everything properly, if I wasn't even an Emoji worthy of graduating?

"Mr. Smiley, I don't know if —"

He cut me off with a wave of his hand. "Think about it," he said. "But consider this. It would be a valuable learning experience for you. I have personally found that I have learned far more about what it means to be an Emoji through teaching than I ever did as a student."

I'm supposed to give him my answer by the end of the week. I think I'm going to do it. Rob moved back to his seat recently, and he and Ally are talking again, but neither one of them talk to me much. I don't see either of them outside of class anymore.

Maybe this is my best shot at graduating.

January 27th, 2016: 8:03 p.m.

I've been helping as Mr. Smiley's aide for over a week now, and it isn't easy. Not that I thought it would be, but the idea of not doing any homework anymore was too tempting to pass up. Although I have come to a pretty unsettling realization after this past week.

Grading is way more work than the actual homework. First of all, Mr. Smiley doesn't give me any answer sheets to use as a reference, so I basically end up having to do the homework, double and triple check to make sure I have the right answer, and try to decide whether or not an illegible scribble counts as correct if it looks enough like the actual answer.

The first batch of homework assignments that I graded had a few unpleasant repercussions. Rob was only one of a few who were less than happy when I handed back the papers.

"60%? But I wrote the same thing down as Ally. What gives, man?"

"I couldn't read more than half of your answers, and for some of the essay questions it looks like you only wrote one or two words."

Rob glowered at me and stuffed the paper away. When I looked around the room there were more unhappy faces. And they knew how to make them, too. You don't know how unsettling it is to be staring at thirty different, unhappy faces made by near-experts. It's one thing when you just see them, but a whole other thing when you know that they're all directed at you.

Mr. Smiley took me aside at the end of that day and talked to me about how I was grading.

"I received more than a few complaints about your grading," he said. "Seems like most of the class thinks that you're being a bit too strict."

"It's not my fault that half of them can't write properly!" I said. I was still stressed out from the previous night spent grading, and not looking forward to the new batch sitting on Mr. Smiley's desk. "I can't tell what most of their answers are. Shouldn't they have to write more clearly?"

Mr. Smiley lowered the reading glasses he sometimes wears and looked at me a moment before answering. It was then that I saw just how tired he was, too. There were lines underneath those perky eyes, and up close his smile looked more strained and forced, as if he was just putting on a face for me. I wondered if it looked the same while he was at home alone, or if he still kept up the facade.

"I think," he began, "that maybe you need to think of a new approach to your position than simply grading homework. For these next few weeks I want you to instead shift your attention to the individual students in the class. You can sit at my desk throughout class. I just want you to observe, and get a good idea of how well everyone is doing, and how much they understand."

"But how is that going to help," I said, "if I still don't know if they're answering the homework questions correctly? Any one of them could just be scribbling down answers. How do I know if they really understand the material?"

"Because that is exactly what I focus on every day during class. Haven't you ever noticed that the class before a homework assignment is due I ask questions that relate to the assignment? And then, at the beginning of the day when the homework is due, I touch briefly on the essentials one more time. Gauge their reactions and confidence, and you will know who to give the benefit of a doubt to."

Then he handed me the next stack of papers to be graded, and I made my way to the transport, and back home again.

That was the first day of my experience being an aide, and I have to say that I think Mr. Smiley is onto something. I've been doing what he said for the past week or so, and I think I'm beginning to notice the things he was talking about.

For instance, Rob is actually a good student. At first I just thought he was a goofball who never pays attention, but when I actually watched him during class, I noticed that he is always listening to what Mr. Smiley says. He doesn't take notes, but his eyes are always focused. Only in between subjects does he ever lean over to someone next to him and whisper some joke to get them laughing. If he's ever called on he always knows the answer.

Most of the class still doesn't like how I grade the papers. They still say that I'm too harsh, or that I made a mistake and they actually knew the answer. I'll only change it if they can explain to me what the correct answer is in their own words, so that I know they really understand. Already I've noticed some of them writing more neatly, too, just so that I can't mark their answer as wrong.

It works for me. I'm not trying to give anyone a bad grade. I only want to do my job as best as I can. In the back of my mind I already know that most everyone will graduate. I'm the only one who doesn't have as good of a chance, so I need to be the one who works harder than all of them. It isn't making my social life any easier, but I think I'm past that now.

I've got to keep pushing myself forward if I want to have any chance. This is maybe my last shot at getting uploaded. I'm the first student Mr. Smiley has ever taken on for a second year, and I don't really think there's any way that he'll keep me for a third.

February 28th, 2016: 3:54 p.m.

The end of the quarter is nearly upon us. After this, there's only one more left until the last one. Before I know it, the end of the year will be here, along with the inevitable finals, performance ratings, and the ending announcements on who passes on to be uploaded, and who stays behind in shame and disgrace.

I remember last year's ceremony too well. It might as well be seared into my memory. I remember sitting there with the rest of my excited classmates. We all passed the final. Back then, there wasn't even a question as to whether or not we would be uploaded or graduate. It was all assumed that we would.

How they did it then was a loud and celebratory ceremony, in which the judges sought to bring about some element of suspense by not releasing the names of the students who would be graduating until the day of the final upload. The idea was to gather the whole class around, and usher them off onto the next major phase in their lives.

They called out our names one by one, but in the end, everyone was standing up on the stage except for me. I remember hearing the muttering and the whispering cascade around the auditorium. Each successive wave hit me with another feeling of shame and self-loathing. I kept my head down throughout the ceremony, and waited until all of the graduates and their families had gone.

There was a touch on my shoulder as I was sitting there, still trying to disappear. When I looked up I saw my mother and father standing over me, both smiling with sad eyes. My mother bent down and hugged me.

"I'm so sorry, sweetie," she said. "If we would have known we wouldn't have gone and put you through all of that."

I wasn't sure if she meant that they shouldn't have put me through the shame of the graduating ceremony, or the decision to send me to school altogether. At that point it didn't make much of a difference to me. I just hugged her back, and then we all went home.

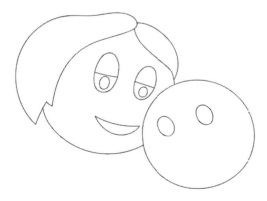

It was only a few weeks before the school year started when I was notified that I could come back for a second year. It came in the form of a digital newsletter, and let me know that given the circumstances, they would allow me to retake the classes that had been offered last year. They called me a special case, but also warned that if I did not pass after this year, they would not grant the same offer again.

I wonder if this year will be any different, seeing as I've stopped taking classes for teaching instead. I wonder if it will give me a better chance of uploading, or if I'll be stuck here forever.

But enough wallowing in my own self-pity and doubt. That only got me to where I am now, and I can't walk down that road any longer.

I've gotten much better at reading my classmates over the last month. I can tell that, for instance, the Seasonals are all over-confident that they will pass, and so they do not try very hard on their homework. I can read pretty much everyone's handwriting now, and I can tell when they're only scribbles. In all honesty, the Seasonals are right. They will all pass. Because at the end of the year, the final exams only matter so much. The only real deciding factor is how well each Emoji does on their expression performance. That's what gets them uploaded. And that's the only thing that I've ever failed at.

Still, they don't hate me anymore. At least, if they do none of them act like it to my face. I think I've earned their respect. And it doesn't hurt that none of them can tell what I'm thinking. That's the one advantage I've noticed about being completely unable to change your expression. You can't betray your feelings except through words. So I stay quiet at Mr. Smiley's desk at the front of the classroom. And I watch. And I listen.

Next quarter Mr. Smiley has told me that he wants me to teach a class myself. He thinks I'll enjoy it, but I'm not a complete fool. I can see that it tires him out to no end, and I know he just wants a break from it himself. Still, I don't think that there's any way that I can convince him to just let me skate by until the end of the year. He's been pushing me harder than anyone else. The stress of failing one of his students must have gotten to him.

So in the end I'm sure that I'll have to do it. Just the thought of it makes my stomach churn, though. There's no way that I can do what Mr. Smiley does. I'm barely getting comfortable with just grading homework and tests, and sitting there at the front of class staring at everyone. I don't even know what I would teach a class on. I hope he'll at least give me one of his own lesson plans to go off of.

I've been trying to practice making different faces in the mirror at home. I try as hard as I can to scrunch up my face, or move my eyes so that they showcase different emotions. But it's no use. The best I can do is blink, wink, or just stare there and bob my head up and down. But I guess any progress is real progress for me at least.

But there isn't much more time left. And if I can't manage to manipulate my features enough to pass the expression performance, then it'll have all been for nothing.

Fourth Quarter

March 4th, 2016: 5:02 p.m.

So today ended up being filled with more surprises than I was expecting. The worst of them all being that Mr. Smiley decided that the first class of the new quarter would be taught by me. This wouldn't have been much of a problem if he had just told me before I walked in the classroom.

"Alright," he said to me. "Today's your day. Hope you're ready."

I stopped in my tracks. "What do you mean?"

Mr. Smiley smiled. "Today's the big day. The class is all yours. I'll just sit at my desk and watch today."

I didn't say anything. I couldn't. I think at that moment my tongue was somewhere in my stomach. The class was filing in behind me and taking their seats. After some amount of time that I lost track of passed, I realized that they were all staring at me, and that I was still there at the front of the room. I set my bag down by the desk, and turned to face my class. I had no idea what I was going to say.

"Okay everyone," I said. I was going to have to wing it. "Today is going to be a little bit different than most classes. First off, I'll be teaching today while Mr. Smiley takes a break. I hope you trust that I know what I'm talking about by now."

A small ripple of nervous laughter floated across the room. I couldn't tell if it was directed at me, or if I had made a good joke. I stared at them until they quieted down. Some shifted in their seats, uneasy by how little I seemed affected by their laughter.

In reality I was panicking inside. My mind raced ahead to come up with some kind of activity to pass the time.

"Let's start the class today with a little warm-up," I said, improvising. "I want everyone to take out a piece of paper and write down their five most favorite expressions that they have made this year so far. Take your time, and when everyone is finished, we'll go around the room and share them."

The students immediately followed my instructions and put their heads down. I looked over at Mr. Smiley and he gave me a thumbs up.

The time I bought with this small activity didn't last long. After not five minutes, most of the heads were raised expectantly, waiting for the next instructions. Once everyone was done I had them all go around and list off their favorites. That soaked up another good ten minutes. By the time we made it all the way around the room I knew what the next jumping off point would be.

"Okay, so we all have our lists. And first I have to say that I think everyone did a really good job coming up with them. Now, I want you to look over your lists and pick the one you think you will display during your expression performance. Remember, you want it to be both unique and important to you. If it isn't you won't be giving it your all, and the judges will notice."

There was a hand raised in the back. One of the Seasonals. She had a jack-o-lantern face that grinned with pointed teeth.

"Yes, in the back," I said.

"No offense," she said. "But are you really the best to be teaching this to us? Shouldn't someone who has passed and graduated be telling us what to do?"

Some of the students started muttering amongst themselves at that. I knew I was at risk of losing the attention and respect of the class. I had to act fast.

"That's a good point," I said. "And I won't lie to you. I didn't pass last year because the judges didn't think my expression was good enough to be uploaded. That's why I had to take this year over."

Nothing but silence. I was aware that they all knew this, and went on.

"However, since I am the only Emoji to go through two years of the academy, I think it's safe to say that I know quite a bit more about what it takes to graduate than most. And I know a lot about what not to do, since they're some of the things that I did do. You learn the best through your mistakes, and I'm only trying to help you all to not make the same ones that I did. Is that a good enough answer for you?"

The jack-o-lantern grin fell a bit slack at the corners. The Seasonal nodded her head. The rest of the class waited.

"Now that that's settled," I said. "I want you to pick your favorite one from your list. Try to get rid of ones you like, and prioritize your final choice over all others. The time for discovering how many expressions you can make is over. You should by now know which one you will take with you once you've uploaded, for it can only be one."

The rest of the class passed smoothly enough. I instructed everyone in the class to practice mastering their chosen expressions. Then I went around and worked with each of them one on one to help them fix their tiny errors and flaws. A misplaced eyebrow or unconvincing smile, anything that would get points docked.

By the end of the day I was exhausted, but it seemed like the class was happy with how the day went. I saw a lot of smiles as they walked out of the room. The snippets of conversation that I heard were all positive and hopeful. I felt a warming sensation rise up to my face that was not unlike pride.

Mr. Smiley held me back after class again and congratulated me. "You've really got a knack for this," he said. "You know, if you don't make the upload again, there will still be a place for you in my classroom."

I thanked him and went home, too tired to think about or try to answer the offer.

So although the day went rather unexpectedly, I'm glad I was surprised with the challenge of teaching my own class. In some ways, I think I would have done a worse job if I had more time to think and plan and worry about it.

Mr. Smiley has been doing this for a long time, I realized, and he just might know what he's doing.

May 23rd, 2016: 6:34 p.m.

Today was the day of the performance exams. I'd been practicing for almost two months to get my angle down. We all waited during class for our turn to go. I was the last name called, and as I stood up and walked out of the classroom, the butterflies were stirring up a tornado in my gut.

I walked down the long hallway until I reached the auditorium. That was where they always had the performance exams. When I walked in, the judges were all sitting in the first row, right in front of the stage. I knew what to do without being told, and took my place at the center of the stage.

"Name," an Emoji with square glasses and red lipstick said. Her head was bent down at the clipboard in her lap. I recognized her as one of the judges from last year, and my stomach dropped.

"Blank," I said.

She looked up and lowered her glasses to take a better look at me. "You took this exam last year," she said. "Did you not?"

I swallowed back the lump in my throat. "Yes, I did."

"I remember," she said, and, leaning over to one of the other judges she spoke loud enough for me to hear, "He didn't pass. This usually doesn't happen. But it should go quick." Then she looked back at me. "You can begin," she said. "Show us your proposed expression."

I stared at them with my blank face. I blinked. I continued to give no sense of expression or emotion. The whole while I was being more true to myself than I ever had been. This was my face, after all. It was the only one I had, and for better or worse I couldn't do anything to change that. I took some little comfort in the knowledge that if I did fail again, I would still have a place here.

After a few moments the lipsticked face spoke up again. "Is that it?" she asked.

I looked right back at her and held my head high. "Yes, and I think that it deserves a place in the next upload."

She sighed. "To be honest with you, Blank, I don't really think that we can support that. I don't want to discourage you, but I think you may be making it harder on yourself by holding out so much hope."

"Now wait," the judge next to her said. "I think we should let him speak his piece first. This is a unique situation. Perhaps he has a good reason for proposing such an expression."

They all looked up at me expectantly. I felt like this was what Mr. Smiley was preparing me for throughout the whole year. He got me better at public speaking and thinking on my feet. And I knew what to say in the moment without hesitating.

"With all due respect," I began, "I believe that a blank expression is just what is needed in the next upload. There are times when we all know exactly what we want to say and how we feel. For those times we employ the use of an expressive Emoji. But there are times when we aren't really sure, or don't know what someone else meant when they said something. In my opinion, the blank expression is best for these occasions. And it can even bring humor to a conversation if used properly."

There was a long moment of silence as I let the words hang in the air. I had said all that I wanted to say on the matter. Now the final decision was out of my hands.

The four heads of the judges converged together and they whispered amongst themselves for some time. I wasn't sure if I was meant to leave, but decided to stay. If they wanted me to go they would dismiss me from the room.

"Well," the lipsticked Emoji finally acknowledged my presence again. "You have brought some important matters to our attention. Rest assured, that we will continue to discuss this amongst ourselves until we arrive at a satisfactory solution."

She waved a hand at me dismissively. "You may go now. You will have our answer come the graduation ceremony like the others."

"If you could please," I said. "Please, let me know if I won't be uploaded before the ceremony. Last year I was the only one who didn't go. I don't think I could go through that again."

The lipsticked Emoji smiled at me from behind her square frames. "Well Blank," she said. "We all must go through trials and tribulations in life. Sometimes that means not getting what we want. But in the end of it all, we each find our own way to make it work. Good luck."

The rest of class was canceled early to give us all a break after the exams. Later this week the final tests would be passed out. I'm not too worried about them. The only thing on my mind is what more the judges could be talking about. Did they only want to tell me that to give me a false sense of hope, or were there some who actually agreed with me, and were fighting for me?

I can only hope that the latter is true, and keep pushing forward. And in the end, if I do fail again, I know that I still have a place by Mr. Smiley's side. Teaching wouldn't be so bad, after all.

June 6th, 2016: 6:15 a.m.: Graduation Day

Today is the day I've been waiting and working for. The transport gets here in another hour, but I just wanted to jot down some final thoughts in case I'm immediately uploaded. This could very well be my last journal post as a student.

The things I have learned from this year include:

1. **The importance of self-discovery.** What helped me to realize this the most, was having a journal to record my thoughts and feelings in. Without it, I could see the events of this year taken in wildly different directions. I might never have agreed to become Mr. Smiley's assistant, and I don't think I would have had the courage to ask Ally out on a date.
2. **The importance of friendship.** Once I became Mr. Smiley's aide, I worked my hardest to repair and rebuild my friendships

with both Rob and Ally. We've restored our friendship to what it was like in the beginning of the year, and I've come to terms with the fact that Ally and I may never be together again. No matter what happens, I want us all to part as friends.

3. **The importance of standing up for what you believe in.** I only discovered this through trial and error. I found that I had to be forced into situations where I was uncomfortable, and scared or nervous in order to actually take a stand on anything. In the past it has been far too easy for me to give up, and claim that whatever making me scared doesn't really matter. The truth is, that it is the only real thing that matters, because it is the one thing standing in your way from getting what you want. I'm still afraid of the same things, and nervous about others, but I can live with that.

4. **The importance of persistence.** Without the ability to continue to push forward in what you know to be right, anyone can fail. You can't rely on ability over hard work and determination, because sometimes your ability isn't valued, and you need to try something else.

As I reflect on these revelations learned throughout this past year, I'm beginning to realize that maybe this is exactly what Mr. Smiley has been trying to teach all of his students every year. I didn't get it the first time, so he took me under his wing so that I could figure it out in my own way.

We had our last class of the year just two days ago. We had another party, a sort of end of the year celebration that was identical to the one we had last year. During it, I took a break from talking with Rob and Ally to go up to Mr. Smiley at his desk.

"Thanks for everything," I said to him. "I don't think I would have gotten this far, or felt as good about myself if it wasn't for everything you've done to help me.

Mr. Smiley gave me his customary grin. "I appreciate that Blank," he said. "And there's also something else that i wanted to talk to you about. I was going to wait until class was dismissed, but I suppose now is as good a time as any."

"What is it?" I was curious.

"I've been told by the judges to let you know that you will have a choice," he said. "If you are accepted into the upload, you don't have to go. I want you to know that."

"Why wouldn't I want to go?" I asked. "That's what every Emoji wants. To be uploaded. What's the point if I have to stay here?"

"The point," Mr. Smiley said, leveling his gaze at me, "is that you, Blank, are not like every other Emoji. You are fundamentally different, and you will be treated as such for as long as you live. I'm sure you already realize this, which is why the judges have asked that I let you know that you do not have to go. If you wish to stay, there will always be a place for you here. I've told you that before, and it hasn't changed."

"Thanks, Mr. Smiley," I said. "I'll think about it."

I haven't talked to him since, but have thought a great deal about what he told me. I still haven't decided what choice I would make, and don't think I will until the time comes. After all, if I'm not accepted then it won't matter either way. I've already experienced what it would be like to be a teacher this year. And I'm okay with that possible future. But begin chosen and uploaded is a whole adventure in and of itself. I'm not sure that I could just walk away from that, just to do what I've been doing this past year over and over for the rest of my life.

June 6th, 2016: 8:00 a.m.: The Ceremony

I brought my notebook with me into the auditorium. We're all here sitting and waiting for them to start calling names. I still haven't decided what I'll do if they call mine.

There goes Ally, first name called. No surprises there. I smiled at her, and gave her the thumbs up when she passed by on her way up to the stage.

One by one, everyone is being called up. I know I'll probably be last again. It feels just like last year. My parents are here up in the stands behind me. I hope they won't be disappointed if I don't make it again.

There goes Rob. Good for him. I knew he would make it too. If I don't join him and Ally, I'm sure they'll start dating. Maybe even have a family together.

There it is! They called my name! Oh my goodness, I'm going. I have to go. I've decided I'm going to take this journal with me, to record my life and experiences on the other side. There will always be time for a life of teaching. Now is my one chance to go after what I want.

And I'm taking it.

One last thing…

First, **thank you** for reading this book! I really appreciate that amongst an ocean of many other books, you chose this one =)

If you enjoyed this book, I would be very grateful if you posted a short review on Amazon. Your support does make a difference and I read every review personally.

If you would like to leave a review, all you need to do is go to this book's page on amazon and click "Write a Customer Review" at the bottom of the page.

Thank you for your support!

Made in the USA
Columbia, SC
16 January 2018